Grace Kerry's
Magic with
Black-Eyed Beans
and other recipes

A Nigerian Cookbook

Published by Amazing Grace Publishers: Established 2004
Photography by: Nduka C. Okoh
Printing: Beacon Printers (Penarth) Ltd. Tel: (029) 2070 8415

This book is dedicated to my mother
for her love so lavishly given over the years
"A mother's love is peace"

ACKNOWLEDGEMENT

I have many people to thank for their support during the production of this cook book, namely, my children, my mother and many friends.

My immeasurable thanks go to my children Nicolette, Nduka, Oge and Dike for unending suggestions, proof reading, correcting and tasting endless recipes. They pointed out omissions and added suggestions. My son Nduka gave many hours to patiently taking the photographs over many weeks and formatting the book by computer.

Many thanks to my friend Gill of "FAN Groups" whose encouragement and energy re-ignited my enthusiasm for finishing this book. Gill also typed the original manuscript, proof-read the work, offered suggestions, tasted almost all the food and even cooked a few!

I'm especially grateful to my mother Mrs. B. U. Kerry who taught me from childhood the art of magical meals and all my friends and colleagues who have tasted my recipes over the years and maintained they were worthy of publication.

I must also thank Gareth of Beacon Printers, Penarth for a job well done.

Finally, my thanks go to all those who will be interested in purchasing this cook book and trying out these delicious recipes.

CONTENTS

Black-eyed beans are an indigenous, very delicious and healthy Nigerian speciality prepared in various forms. It has been the main source of protein in many of our local communities for generations.

There are three basic recipes made with black-eyed beans; Ewa, Moi Moi and Akara (illustrated on the pages that follow). These basic ways of using the beans lend themselves to endless variations, some of which are included in this cook book, and some I'm sure you will create yourself.

1)   Ewa uses the beans washed and straight from the packet.

2)   Moi Moi and Akara use de-husked beans. For best results, the de-husking involves soaking the beans for at least four hours, or overnight and rubbing the surface husk or shell off to leave the cream bean which is inside. This takes a bit of time, but can be done with children or friends, or while watching television and can be fun. I find it soothing to do!

There is generally a lack of knowledge in the UK about African, and particularly Nigerian, cuisine. Black-eyed beans are probably the most nutritious and common ingredient of Nigerian cooking. This authentic indigenous food is surprisingly easy to prepare. Some people don't know what to do with black-eyed beans but these are the recipes I grew up with! For a long time, I have wanted to share the benefits of this wonderful food with people from other cultures. Now modern cooking implements make these exciting new flavours easy to create in a fraction of the original time! This scrumptious cuisine captures the magic of Nigerian cooking which I learned at my mother's knee. It is tempting, tasty, and suitable for all occasions. It is best served hot, although equally delicious as a cold snack or if you are in a hurry.

I have interspersed these black-eyed beans recipes with other recipes which my friends love, such as, corn and plantain cuisine, and my classic delicious style of Nigerian stew, together, they illustrate the richness and versatility of the Nigerian diet.

I have also deliberately used the teacup for measurement to save the worry or uncertainty of the metric measurement. Everything should be cooked on medium heat but heat should be reduced to simmer food.

Black-eyed beans are a nutritious cheap source of protein, complex carbohydrates, iron, and calcium and give enough steady energy to ground you throughout the day. Traditionally, palm oil (extracted from palm nuts, which grow on certain varieties of palm trees) is used to cook them, which gives the dishes a beautiful deep yellow glow/colour and a tasty nutty flavour. Palm oil is relatively easy to find (in Asian and Afro-Caribbean shops) but in the absence of palm oil, any healthy oil such as olive oil will do.

Dry, ground black-eyed beans (which look just like wheat flour) can also be purchased from any Afro-Caribbean or Asian shop, especially in London. Note however that the beans may have been ground with the husk in tact and may not produce quite so authentic a taste as when you de-husk them yourself.

The magic of black-eyed beans is that the dishes are versatile and can be eaten as a main meal, a side dish, or as a snack; and they taste even better the following day!

Finally, note that when making the recipes some ingredients may be substituted or removed to suit specific tastes and diets, for example meat or eggs instead of fish or prawns. This is particularly true of chilli peppers. In Nigeria we like the dishes hot and I might use one of the very hot scotch bonnet chillies if I am cooking for the family. However many people in Britain are likely to prefer to use a less strong chilli, or half a red scotch bonnet. For milder flavour, remove seeds from chillies.

EWA

(Do not de-husk beans)
Serves 4

Ingredients

Black-eyed beans . . . . .1½ teacups
Palm oil or any cooking oil . . . . .½ tea cup
Onion . . . . .1 (small)
Fish or vegetable stock . . . . .¾
Fresh basil & coriander . . . . .1 leaf each
Thyme . . . . .1 sprig
Garlic . . . . .1 small clove
Eggs 2
Chilli pepper if preferred
A few fresh prawns or small fresh fish fillet
Salt to taste

Cooking method

- Wash beans and pour into average saucepan with beans well covered with hot water.
- Boil for 15 minutes. Drain and rinse with hot water.
- Return to pan and replace with boiled water.
- Add a little salt and continue to cook on medium heat for another 40 minutes.
- Keep topping up water until the beans are cooked and tender, with little water left.
- Chop the onion and set aside. Add the palm oil to the beans.
- Pop stock cube into the beans.
- Blend all the other ingredients but not the sea food and set aside.
- Stir the chopped onion, seafood and all ingredients into the cooked beans to give a thick but moist consistency. Break the eggs, whisk and add to the beans.
- Cover and simmer for about 10 minutes.
- Serve with vegetable salad or plain rice.

This is a family favourite! You must try this as beans on toast for breakfast but please do not forget to go to work!

MOI MOI

(De-husk beans)
Serves 4

Ingredients

Black-eyed beans . . . . .1½ teacups (8oz/200g)
Onion . . . . .1 small size
Red pepper (hot scotch bonnet) . . . . .½ or 1 (if you like it hot!)
Thyme . . . . .1 sprig
Palm oil or any cooking oil . . . . .½ teacup
Eggs 2
Prawns (optional) . . . . .a small cup
Meat lovers could add some corned beef
Basil . . . . .1 leaf
Vegetable stock cube . . . . .1 (or salt to taste)
Foil dishes, freezer bags or plastic microwave containers.

Cooking method

- For fast and easy de-husking soak beans in boiling water for 30-60 mins and de-husk for most authentic result. Rinse under tap, removing husks as they float to the surface. To save time you may use ground beans.
- Add the chopped onion, red pepper, herbs and all ingredients to the de-husked (or ground) beans with one stock cube dissolved in a little hot water and blend.
- If the mixture is too thick add a little warm water. The mixture should be of a thick slightly runny consistency.
- Add cooking oil to the mixture and stir.
- Scoop the mixture into appropriate containers.
- To steam, boil one pint of water in a large pot and place containers with mixtures carefully in water so the water does not overlap the sides of the dishes and steam for 15-20 minutes (depending on size of container). The result should resemble a moist sponge cake.
- Alternatively, cook in average microwave containers for about 6 minutes. Steaming however produces the best result!
- When cooked cut this nutritious savoury cake in slices and serve with rice or vegetables (cooked or fresh).

Everyone should try this dish; once tried, it's never forgotten!

**This is a festive favourite in Nigeria and it's often served
on special occasions. It is also excellent for those convalescing
from illness as it is highly nutritious and easily digestible.**

AKARA PANCAKES

(De-husk beans)
Serves 4

Ingredients

Black-eyed beans . . . . .1¼ cup
Onion . . . . .1small size
Palm Oil or any cooking oil . . . . .¼ cup
Fresh basil . . . . .1 leaf
Fresh coriander . . . . .1 leaf
Fresh thyme . . . . .1 sprig
Garlic . . . . .½ small clove
Vegetable stock cube . . . . .1 dissolved in a little hot water
Extra oil for frying
Water if needed (Often not needed)
Salt to taste
Two fresh eggs may be added for extra creaminess but the mixture is still
delicious on its own.
Fresh whole prawns may also be added for variety and flavour.

Cooking method

- For fast and easy de-husking soak beans in boiling water for 30-60 mins. De-husk. Rinse under tap, removing husks as they float to the surface.
- Blend with all the other ingredients (except the prawns).
- Allow to stand for 10-15 minutes. Add prawns and mix again. Mixture should be thick and runny.
- Pour a little oil in frying pan. Heat until hot.
- Scoop paste with ladle into the hot oil to form pancakes. Best fried 3 or 4 at a time.
- Turn pancakes when golden brown on the under side. Take care to keep them from sticking together. If they do stick separate with a spatula when cooked. Place on paper towel-lined dish for a few minutes to absorb excess oil.
- Sprinkle with black pepper to serve. Best eaten hot.

Serve with salad as snack or appetizer. Unbelievably delicious!

AKARA WITH KING PRAWNS

(De-husk beans)
Serves 4

Ingredients

Black-eyed beans . . . . .1 teacup
Onion . . . . .1 small
Palm oil or any healthy cooking oil . . . . .Enough for deep frying
Egg 1
King Prawns (or Tiger Prawns if you're feeling flash!) . . . .5 - 8
Vegetable or fish stock cube . . . . .1 cube dissolved in little hot water
Basil and coriander . . . . .2 leaves each
Fresh thyme . . . . .A small spray
Garlic . . . . .1 small clove
Chilli (optional) . . . . .½
Salt to taste
A teaspoon of butter

Cooking method

- For fast and easy de-husking soak beans in boiling water for 30-60 mins. De-husk. Rinse under tap, removing husks as they float to the surface. Set aside.
- Shell the prawns, removing the heads and tails, and set aside.
- Dissolve a quarter of vegetable stock in a little hot water.
- Add to prawns with two rings of chopped onions and cook in a small pot on low heat for 10 minutes. Set aside.
- Meanwhile blend all remaining ingredients including beans together into a thick paste. Add a little palm oil for colour.
- Add the butter and mix gently with a wooden spoon.
- Heat oil in a deep pan until very hot.
- Use a ladle to scoop. Add a prawn to a scoop of mixture and place slowly in hot oil to fry until golden brown.
- This should form balls of akara encasing the prawns.

Absolutely delicious! Serve with "Grace's Rich Vegetable Salad."

AUBERGINE FLAT BEAN CAKE

(De-husk beans)
Serves 4

Ingredients

Black-eyed beans . . . . .1 tea-cup

Onion . . . . .1 small size

Fresh thyme . . . . .1 sprig

Palm oil or any other cooking oil . . . . .Enough for shallow frying

Eggs 2

Aubergine . . . . .½ small, sliced into 1mm discs

Water, if needed . . . . .¼ cup

Vegetable or fish stock cube . . . . ½ dissolved in a little hot water

Basil and coriander . . . . .1 leaf each

Garlic . . . . .1 small clove

Chilli (optional) . . . . .½

1 medium red chilli, if you like it hot

Salt to taste

Cooking method

- For fast and easy de-husking soak beans in boiling water for 30-60 mins. De-husk. Rinse under tap, removing husks as they float to the surface. Or use pre-ground beans.
- Chop onions, red pepper, herbs and blend together with the stock cube.
- Add beans and blend again. Add a table spoon of cooking oil and mix well. Set aside.
- Cut aubergine into 1mm discs, fry in shallow oil until golden brown on both sides and set aside.
- Add more oil into pan if needed and heat until very hot. Scoop bean mix with ladle into hot oil. Add a disc of aubergine to each scoop and place in hot oil.
- Fry until golden brown on both sides, turning with spatula.
- Serve for breakfast or at any time.

Scrumptious!

MAMA'S DELIGHT

(Do not de-husk beans)
Serves 4

Ingredients

Black-eyed beans	1¼ cups
Onion	1 medium
Vegetable stock cube	1 Dissolved in hot water
Palm oil or olive oil	¾ cup
Ripe plantain (but not over-ripe)	1 small
Preferred tinned fish (tuna, salmon or sardine)	1 small tin
Garlic	1 small clove
Red chilli pepper, if preferred	
Salt to taste	
A sprig of thyme & coriander and 2 leaves of basil	

Cooking method

- Wash beans and pour into average saucepan with enough hot water to cover the beans. Boil for 15 minutes. Drain and rinse with hot water. Return to pan and add boiled water to cover beans. Add a little salt and cook for another 40 minutes.
- Keep adding water until beans are cooked and nearly dry to give a thick but moist consistency. Add the oil and stir gently.
- Blend all ingredients (herbs, garlic, stock cube ,etc) together, except the tinned fish, onion and plantain.
- Chop onion into small pieces and set aside.
- Cut plantain into 6 round pieces and set aside.
- Finally, add all ingredients including onions and plantain to the cooked beans and stir gently.
- Simmer for 10-15 minutes
- **Bingo, and there you have it!**

Serve with salad or on its own

BEANS AND COCONUT RICE

(Do not de-husk beans)
Serves 6

Ingredients

Black eyed beans . . . . .1 cup (Cook as for Ewa)

Whole coconut . . . . .1 or 2 cups of unsweetened desiccated coconut

Vegetable or fish stock cube . . . . .1 (for the rice)

Palm oil or preferred cooking oil. . . . . .¼ cup

Basmati rice . . . . .2 cups

Olive oil . . . . .½ cup

Fresh fish fillets (any) . . . . .4 small pieces

Thyme . . . . .A sprig

Basil & coriander . . . . .2 leaves each

Onion . . . . .2 medium

Garlic . . . . .1 small clove

Salt to taste

Cooking method

"Coconut Rice"

- Break coconut and discard the outer shells.
- Meanwhile soak the rice in cold water for 20-30 minutes, wash and set aside.
- Grate or crush the flesh of the whole coconut. Pour grated coconut into 1 pint of boiled water.
- Stand for ten minutes and strain through cheesecloth. Alternatively, unsweetened desiccated coconut may be used. Dissolve one stock cube and add to the coconut milk.
- Pour into a container and set aside. Blend half the fresh herbs with garlic and add to the coconut milk. Chop one onion and set aside.
- Meanwhile ,pour the olive oil into a cooking pot and heat until very hot.
- Fry the chopped onion with a sprinkle of salt until soft or golden brown.
- Pour the coconut milk mixture and then the rice into the fried onion.
- Mix and simmer on low gas in the coconut milk until rice is cooked and all juice absorbed into the rice.

"Fish and Beans": To accompany the Coconut Rice dish.

- Cook beans as for Ewa until soft.
- Remember the beans must be cooked until very soft; and should disintegrate when pressed between fingers.
- Keep adding water until tender and to give thick consistency.
- Blend the remaining red chilli pepper (if required), basil, coriander and thyme together. Chop the second onion and add (with all ingredients) to cooked beans and mix carefully.
- Now add the fish fillets and the cooked ingredients. Stir well and simmer for 15 minutes.
- **Serve the "Fish and Beans" with the "Coconut Rice" and wait for the compliments!**

This is truly unbelievable! Watch people ask for second
and third helpings of this tasty dish!
You could add a dash of fresh vegetables to serve.

BEANS WITH YAM

(Do not de-husk beans)
Serves 4

Ingredients

Black-eyed beans . . . . .1 cup
Yam (Ghana or Puna Yam is heavenly) . . . . .4 small pieces (6cm sq)
Tomatoes . . . . .1 fresh
Onion . . . . .1 small
Palm oil or any healthy cooking oil . . . . .½ teacup
Vegetable stock cube 1
Garlic . . . . .Small clove
Water . . . . .½ pint to start with
Fresh Basil, Thyme and Coriander . . . . .A leaf or sprig of each
1 red chilli pepper (optional)
Salt to taste

Cooking method

- Cook beans as for Ewa until soft.
- Blend all ingredients and add to cooked beans.
- Peel off rough outer skin of yam, cut into squares or rounds of about 4 centimetres in diameter. Wash and add to cooked beans. Stir in the oil.
- Mix and simmer for a further 15 minutes or until yam is cooked or soft.
- Serve on its own or with vegetable salad.

This is truly out of this world! It is my mother's favourite. She believes it is the cure for all sadness.

SAVOURY SPINACH BEAN CAKE

(De-husk beans)
Serves 4

Ingredients

Black-eyed beans . . . . .1 cup
Onion . . . . .1 small size
Basil & coriander leaves .1 leaf each.
Thyme . . . . .1 sprig
Vegetable stock cube . . . . .1 dissolved in a little hot water
Garlic . . . . .1 small clove
Eggs 2
Baby spinach . . . . .8 leaves or as preferred
Palm oil or any healthy cooking oil . . . . .¼ cup
Red chilli pepper (optional)
Tin foil dishes, freezer bags, or microwave containers.
Prawn may be added for variety and extra flavour.

Cooking method

- For fast and easy de-husking soak beans in boiling water for 30-60 mins. De-husk. Rinse under tap, removing husks as they float to the surface. You may use pre-ground beans.
- Chop onion and red chilli pepper and blend in blender with herbs.
- Add the de-husked beans and dissolved stock cube and blend again.
- Add eggs and garlic and blend. Stir in the oil. Wash spinach, soak in boiled water for 10 minutes, drain and chop.
- Add to the mixture and stir in well.
- Scoop mixture into appropriate containers, cover and set aside.
- Boil two pints of water in a medium pot.
- Place containers with mixture in the pot. Take care water does not spill over into the mixture.
- Steam for about 15-20 minutes until it firms up like a light sponge cake.
- Or alternatively cook in the microwave for 6 minutes.
- **This dish however is best steamed!**
- Serve hot with rice and vegetables, as a main or side dish.

This dish has an amazingly light flavour which
is enhanced by the spinach. Perfect for a
vegetarian picnic on a spring day, or for a summer barbecue.

BEANS WITH SWEET CORN

(Do not de-husk beans)
Serves 4

Ingredients

Black-eyed beans . . . . .1 cup
Sweet corn . . . . .medium tin
Prawns (or fresh fish) . . . . .a tea cup
Onion . . . . .1 medium
Basil and coriander . . . . .1 leaf each
Thyme . . . . .1 sprig
Vegetable stock cube 1
Garlic . . . . .small clove
Palm oil or any healthy cooking oil . . . . .½ cup
Salt to taste

Cooking method

- Follow the Ewa recipe until beans are cooked and almost dry.
- Chop the onion and set aside.
- Blend all the ingredients (except prawns and sweet corn) in a blender
- Stir in the oil and all ingredients including dissolved stock cube into the cooked beans and mix.
- Add the prawns and sweet-corn.
- Combine the whole mix gently to give a thick moist consistency.
- Cover and simmer for 10 minutes.
- Serve with rice, or vegetable salad.

This is irresistible!
Corn is delicious with black-eyed beans at all times
and adds to its nourishing qualities.

MOI MOI DELUXE

(De-husk beans)
Serves 4

Ingredients

Black-eyed beans . . . . .1 cup (de-husked)
Onions . . . . .1 small
Palm oil or any healthy oil . . . . .½ cup
Eggs 3
Prawns . . . . .1 cup
Basil and coriander . . . . .1 leaf each
Thyme . . . . .1 sprig
Tomatoes . . . . .1 medium
Diced mixed vegetables .1 cup (broccoli, charlotte,
corn, and courgette)

Vegetable stock cube 1
Garlic . . . . .¼ clove
Thick cream . . . . .2 teaspoons
Salt to taste
Average sized sandwich or baking pan

Cooking method

- For fast and easy de-husking soak beans in boiling water for 30-60 mins. De-husk. Rinse under tap, removing husks as they float to the surface. Set prawns aside and do not blend. Add the 2 eggs with other ingredients into de-husked beans and blend. Set aside.
- Rub the baking dish with butter or margarine and set aside.
- Dice vegetables and steam in a little stock juice for 5 minutes until water is absorbed.
- Add diced vegetables to bean mixture. Mix thoroughly and transfer into the baking dish.
- Whisk the remaining one egg into the cream and pour evenly on the pastry but do not mix.
- Slice the fresh tomato into rounds and decorate the pastry with it.
- Cover and bake in medium preheated oven for 20 minutes.
- Serve with cooked rice or on its own.

My friends love this recipe!

FRIED PLANTAIN WITH EWA

Serves 4

Ingredients

Ripe Plantain (but not too ripe) 1
Cooking oil . . . . .Enough for shallow or
deep frying
Black pepper . . . . .A sprinkle
Ready prepared Ewa . . . . .For 4 people

Cooking method

- Remove or peel the outer skin of the ripe plantain
- Slice plantain in slants into 1 cm rings
- Heat oil in a frying pan until hot.
- Fry the plantain a few at a time in hot shallow oil, or all together in deep oil.
- Fry until golden brown turning with a spatula, fork or large spoon.
- When ready sprinkle with black pepper and serve on its own or with vegetables.
- Plantain is healthy eating because, for instance, it does not absorb oil when fried.

This is excellent for digestion and Children thrive on this. See what happens when you serve it at one of their birthday parties!

PLANTAIN DUMPLING

Serves 6

Ingredients

Very ripe plantain . . . . .2 large
Eggs 3
Fresh basil ,& coriander . . . . .1 leaf each
Thyme . . . . .1 sprig
Onion . . . . .1 small
Garlic . . . . .½ Small clove
Plain flour . . . . .A teacup

Tomato . . . . .1 small
Palm Oil or preferred cooking oil . . . . .1 cup
Salt to taste.
Baking powder . . . . .2 teaspoons
Foil or freezer bags/containers.

Cooking method

- First, remove the outer skin of the plantains.
- Chop plantains and blend into a soft dough. Add the flour and baking powder and mix.
- Chop the onions and blend with the rest of the ingredients
- Stir all ground ingredients into the plantain dough and mix well. This should be of a thick runny consistency, like for a sponge cake. Add warm water if needed. Set aside.
- Pour 2 pints of water into a large pot and bring to boil.
- Meanwhile transfer the mixture into foil or freezer containers and seal. Place the containers in the pot and steam for 50 minutes. Pot must not boil dry, so top up water when necessary.

Serve with rice, vegetables or with cream as a dessert.

This is a local favourite!
Its sweet taste is a cunning mixture of soothing and exotic.

FLAT CORN CAKES

Serves 4

Ingredients

Corn . . . . .3 cobs or a large tin of corn
Eggs 2
Cooking oil . . . . .Enough for shallow frying
Fresh basil, & coriander .A leaf each
Thyme . . . . .A sprig
Baking Powder . . . . .2 level teaspoons
Vegetable or fish stock cube 1
Prawns . . . . .½ cup
Plain flour . . . . .1 level teacup
Garlic . . . . .½ small clove
Salt to taste
A drop of palm oil, if available, for colour
A little chilli

Cooking method

- Strip the corn kernels from cob or drain tinned corn and pour into blender. Set the prawn aside and do not blend.
- Add all the other ingredients including the palm oil into the blender and blend. Pour into a clean bowl. Add the prawns and mix with wooden spoon.
- Heat oil in a frying pan until very hot.
- Using a ladle scoop the mixture, a bit at a time into the hot oil until golden brown on each side turning with a spatula.
- **These cakes are as easy to prepare as they are delicious!**

**The final result should resemble a flat tea cake
and they are excellent for parties.
Serve with rice, fresh salad or as a snack.**

BEANS WITH SALMON

(Do not de-husk beans)
Serves 4

Ingredients

Black-eyed beans	1½ cups
Onion	2 small
A Slice of red chilli pepper (optional)	1, if you like it hot
Vegetable stock cube	2
Palm oil or preferred cooking oil	cup
Basil, and coriander	1 leaf of each
Thyme	1 sprig
Salmon fish fillet	1 large
Curry powder	teaspoon
Garlic	clove

Cooking method

- Cook beans as for Ewa until soft.
- Chop one onion, pepper, herbs and blend. Set aside. Blend only one onion.
- Cut salmon fillet into 4 pieces and steam with a little stock cube in little water for 10 minutes. Set aside.
- Add oil, and the other chopped onion and all ingredients including curry powder to beans and mix well. Add the steamed fish and mix once more.
- Cover and simmer for 10 minutes.

Serve with basmati rice, cooked or fresh vegetables for a lip smacking taste and satisfaction!

GRACE'S RICH VEGETABLE SALAD

Serves any number

Ingredients

Lettuce, Cabbage, Celery, Tomatoes,

Spring Onions, Cucumber & Carrots

Baked beans (preferably Heinz)

Favoured tinned fish . . . . .A small tin to serve 4

Avocado . . . . .½ of one to serve 4

Eggs to decorate . . . . .2 to serve 4

Olive oil . . . . .1 tablespoon to serve 4

Salad Cream . . . . .1 teaspoon to serve 4

Watercress to garnish

Grated Cheese . . . . .A sprinkle

Cooking method

- Wash all vegetables in cold water. Leave in a large sieve to drain dry, or pat dry with paper kitchen towel.
- Chop, slice or shred all vegetables.
- Set all other ingredients aside. Boil eggs, quarter and set aside.
- Transfer all ingredients, except the eggs into a large salad bowl.
- Gently mix with wooden spoon to incorporate or combine all ingredients thoroughly. Decorate with peeled and quartered boiled eggs and sprinkle with grated cheese. Garnish with watercress.
- **And that's it!**
- Serve with rice, moi moi or akara.

This vegetable salad is in a class of its own!

MY STEW

Serves 4-6

Ingredients

Lamb cutlets 6
Chicken thighs or drumsticks 6
Fresh Salmon . . . . .3 small fillets
Plum Tomatoes . . . . .1 tin
Vegetable or fish stock cube . . . . .1 ½
Onions . . . . .2 medium size
Olive oil or any preferred cooking oil . . . . .1 cup
Coriander & Basil . . . . .3 leaves each
Thyme . . . . .A sprig
Medium/hot curry powder . . . . .1 level dessertspoon
Red chilli pepper (scotch bonnet) . . . . .Half, or as preferred
Garlic . . . . .1 small Clove
Normal large red pepper (Capsicum)
Salt to taste

Cooking method

- First, boil the meat with one chopped onion, half the herbs, a little water and salt for 20 minutes and set aside. Meat must be cooked or steamed until almost all the meat stock has been absorbed.
- Meanwhile, peel and chop the garlic with the second onion and set aside. Blend the tinned tomatoes with the remaining coriander, basil, thyme and large red pepper together and set aside. If you fancy a hot meal add half the scotch bonnet red chilli pepper (or a whole one if you like it very hot!) and blend again.
- Next, heat the cooking oil in a medium saucepan until hot. Fry the chopped onion and garlic until soft or golden brown. Now pour the ground ingredients into the fried onion. Add the stock cube and the curry powder and stir gently. Cover and simmer for 5 minutes.
- Pour in the cooked meat with it's stock. Stir again, cover and simmer for 30 minutes until the stew thickens and the oil settles at the top.
- On the other hand, a quick stew can be made by frying the onions and garlic first until soft. Then add all the ground ingredients and the fresh meat into the pot of fried onions at once, cover and simmer on low heat for 40 minutes. Add the fish10mins to the end.
- **To make fish stew without meat, add the seafood after the stew has been cooking for only 10 minutes and simmer for another 15 minutes.**

This meal is truly wicked, especially with coconut rice!
It is also delicious with fried plantain, cooked yam,
boiled potatoes, cooked beans, and even spaghetti and pasta!

MOI MOI EXTRA

(De-husk beans)
Serves 4-6

Ingredients

Black-eyed beans	1 cup
Very ripe plantain	1 medium
Tinned corn	Medium tin
Palm oil or any cooking oil	½ cup
Prawn	1 cup
Tomato	1 small
Eggs	2
Pain flour	¾ cup
Baking powder	2 teaspoons
Fresh basil and coriander	2 leaves each
Fresh thyme	A sprig
Onion	1 small
Garlic	1 small clove
Salt to taste	
Foil containers or freezer bags.	

Cooking method

- For fast and easy de-husking soak beans in boiling water for 30-60 mins. De-husk. Rinse under tap, removing husks as they float to the surface.
- Peel and chop onion and blend with the rest of the ingredients (except the prawns and eggs) and set aside.
- Next, blend the de-husked beans, corn and plantain together. Set aside.
- Add all the other ingredients to this mixture and blend again.
- Add a little warm water (if necessary) to this mixture and blend again to form a thick runny consistency.
- Now add the prawns, whisked eggs, dissolved stock cube and oil to the mixture and stir gently. Set aside.
- Pour 2 pints of water into a medium sized pot and bring to the boil.
- Using a ladle, scoop mixture into containers, cover, place in pot, cover pot and steam for 40 minutes.
- Cut up to serve
- Serve alone or with vegetable salad.

It looks good, it tastes good and it really does you good!

ABOUT THE AUTHOR

Dr Grace Kerry has a Ph.D in Special Educational Needs and M.Ed in Educational Psychology. She has taught for many years as a University lecturer and as an Advisory teacher for Teaching English as a Second Language in primary and secondary schools.

Dr Kerry was taught from an early age by her mother and grand mother to appreciate the endless and exciting possibilities of Nigerian cooking. She has many interests but loves cooking and her healthy meals have been enjoyed by family and friends for many years.

Notes

Notes

Notes

Notes